Passive Income Ideas
for Beginners

60 Proven Ways to Make Money
and Free Yourself from the
Regular 9 to 5

Table of Contents

Introduction

I want to thank you for choosing this book, 'Passive Income Ideas for Beginners - 60 Proven Ways to Make Money and Free Yourself from the Regular 9 to 5'.

How many of you have heard the term "passive income" and wondered if it's too good to be true? Have you always wanted to take a shot at it, but didn't think it's worth the effort? Well, this guide is about to bust your misconceptions about passive income. Passive income has become the Holy Grail for a lot of people who wish to market themselves online. And why not? After all, it's effortless, isn't it? I am going to be honest with you here. It's not exactly effortless, at least not at first. It's going to take some time and effort to get your idea rolling. It could even be grueling initially depending upon the passive income method you pick but, I promise you, as time passes by and you continue to give your best, money will start flowing in and the real magic will start to happen.

For most of us, passive income is a means to escape the proverbial rat race. To me, it equates to complete freedom and a way to achieve some solid financial independence. Passive income is also a sort of extrication from the shackles of the 9 to 5 corporate job. If your corporate job has been sucking the life out of you, then here's your chance to get unleashed. Over the years, I have realized that binding yourself with extra work is not only enslaving, but it also poses as a huge hindrance to true happiness. Having the total freedom to work, live and roam as per leisure is no longer an impossible dream.

If you are a hustler, I have some mind-blowing and realistic passive income ideas for you. I have described each passive idea in detail, along with crisp information about how you can get started and how much you can approximately earn from it. This book also has a cool 30-day passive income starter challenge that can help you learn exactly how to go about establishing your financial independence through passive income. Happy Reading!!

CHAPTER ONE

60 Passive Income Ideas

Get Paid to Switch on Your Computer

Who would have thought that merely turning on your computer could earn you some money? I know it sounds crazy, but it's real. There are several companies out there in the market who will pay you for sharing the processing power of your computer. Now, you will certainly not make a lot of money, but you won't be putting in any effort either. All you are required to do is download software that will keep working in the background without impacting the speed or quality of your Internet. All of these companies have a very active response system, which is always there to help you in case any issues crop up.

You can sign up on websites such as Gomez peers or a Distributed cloud network to start earning your money through your computer's processing power. You can expect to get paid anywhere between $0.10 and $40 per hour as per the service provider you are using. Yeah, that sounds like peanuts, but think about it… you aren't doing anything more than signing up for an app and downloading their software that doesn't take more than a minute. Isn't it a decent deal?

Invest in Dividend Stocks

This is one of the most tried and tested ways of earning yourself a passive income on the side. You need to invest a small amount of money upfront without any guarantee that it will help you make any further cash. Now that sounds a little risky, but if you get the hang of the system, you might start making some good money, and if you do, then I promise that it could be one of the most profitable ventures in the market.

How do you make money? Companies reward all their shareholders with regular dividends in cash generally after every quarter. Now, this particular passive income idea may need a lot of research before you get started. You may have to spend a few days researching how the stock market works and which companies are worth investing in. How much can you earn? If you invest a total of $2,500 in about 50 shares of a company, each costing $50, then during the first year, you will get paid 2.5% as dividend. This will earn you a dividend income of $62.50. If you wish to make large sums of money, then you need to invest more so you can receive larger dividends.

Create an App

Apps are an extremely popular means of making money. If you have a little app- developing knowledge, then you can make huge amounts of profit if you make your own and sell it. There are different kinds of apps that you can sell, including fitness apps, productivity apps, cooking apps, gaming apps, or apps that will also pay to perform various tasks. How does one get started? If you have some technical skills, you can create an app or simply hire an expert who can create one for you. There are so many technical experts who can create an app for you at affordable prices.

Creating an app might require a lot of time and effort, but once you have created an app, you can sell it in an app store and make good money out of it. One can make even up to thousands of dollars every month by selling apps. As per the statistics, about 25% of developers in the iOS store are earning as high as $5,000 every month. Of course for you to earn that kind of money is going to take some time, but it's a great indication of how much money one can make if they take this idea seriously.

Invest in Real Estate

Investing in real estate isn't as much of a hassle as many think. In fact, it could be an incredibly profitable venture. If you put in a little bit of time, effort and money at the start, you can sit back and see the money roll in within a short period of time. So, how do you get started? For starters, you will have to purchase property, and then start renting it out. Soon, you will start earning a steady flow of income every month in the form of rent. You, as a landlord, may have a few responsibilities such as handling the maintenance, fixing repairs if any and collecting rent each month.

If you are short on cash, you can consider investing in crowd-fund real estate. You can use a crowd-funding platform like Fundraise and start with investing as little as $500. How much will you earn? Your income totally depends upon how much you have invested in the property and the locality it is set in. If you have a rental property without any mortgage on it, then you will not only make a lot of money through rent, but you can also get to keep all the money.

Start Your Own Blog and Monetize It

You must have been surfing through a lot of blogs every day, but do you know that you can make your own blog and earn some money too? There are so many bloggers out there who are making a full-time income out of their blogs, and you don't need to be a rocket scientist to start your own blog. You can pick a topic that you have some good knowledge about and create a website for yourself around that topic.

How do you monetize your blog?

Again, this is simpler than you think.

- Start adding affiliate posts to your blog posts.

- Write some sponsored content – write for companies or a brand, which will pay you to write about their products and services.

- Get some ads to know your websites by signing up for ad network programs such as Google AdSense.

How much can you earn? It depends on how much content you post, the kind of viewership you have, ads, sponsored content and the amount of traffic you receive. Traffic is an important aspect of money-making through blogs. The more the visitors, the higher will be your chances of making money.

Sell Stock Photos

Raise your hand if you have awesome photography skills! But how will it help you make money? You can simply sell your photos online. All you have to do is click some good pictures, edit them well, upload them online and earn money every time someone views and downloads it. Isn't that cool? The best part about this gig is that you don't even have to set a website to sell the photos. There are several platforms online which will help you sell the photographs. How do you get started? Just use your smartphone camera or a DSLR camera to take some decent photos and upload them online on websites like iStockphoto, Shutterstock, Snapwire, Alamy and many more.

How much can you earn?

- If you sign up on iStockphoto, your commission will range in between 15% to 45%. You can typically earn about $1-$20 every image.

- If you use Dreamstime, you can earn anywhere between $1-$40 for each image plus the royalties – between 25-50%.

Certain websites can get $100 plus, while the others may not help you earn more than a dollar. The number of people purchasing your photograph is extremely important for your income; therefore, try and get as much traffic to your photos as possible.

Become an Author on Kindle

Over 10 years ago, if someone wished to become an author, they had to hire an agent and publisher to be able to even consider selling a book. The times have changed for the better, and, today, you, and almost anyone, regardless of their experience, can become an established author. With platforms like Amazon Kindle, it has become extremely easy to publish your own book and make money from it. One of the best things about publishing a book online is that you can work with your own timeline without having to put in too much money to get started.

The first step towards becoming an author on Kindle is to choose whether you want to write something fictional or non-fictional, and then pick a topic which not only matches this genre, but also something that you have good knowledge about, and then start writing a book. How much can you earn? Through Kindle direct publishing, you can earn between 35% - 70% royalties. Sometimes, the author may get paid a specific amount per book such as $2 or $3 regardless of the original price of the book. How much you can make through books completely depends on the number of copies you sell, so, don't forget to market yourself well.

Shop on Cashback Websites

If you have been using a credit card, you know that many credit card companies offer cashback each time you shop for something online, and that's not the only method of getting cashback on your purchases. In fact, you can get cashback on the purchases you make from cashback websites too. If you are someone who mostly shops online, you are going to be saving yourself some huge cash by using these cashback websites. How does it work? It's really simple. You make a purchase online by browsing through your favourite shopping portals. Such websites may include famous brands, retailers and even stores like Target or Macy's. In return for these purchases, the shopping portals share their commission with the users in the form of cash backs.

You can simply use portals such as Mr. Rebates, Ebates, Pennyful, TopCashback and many more to get started. How much can you earn? If you frequently shop online, then the chances are that you will get high cash back each month. Earning money through cash backs may not seem like you are actually earning anything, but you will do yourself a huge favor by saving yourself a lot of money from your purchases.

Become an Airbnb Host

Do you have a big house or a spare room in your apartment? If you do, then get ready to earn some cash by renting it out. What is Airbnb? It's a website that allows the homeowners to rent out their apartments to people who need to rent a place for a few days instead of staying at a hotel. One can make a lot of money by merely renting out a room in their house. How do you get started? Simply create an account on the Airbnb website and then list your property. Soon, you will have guests sending you a request for booking a stay. Once you have chosen to accept their request, then you can receive the payment from them as soon as they check in.

How much do you earn? Renting out your property through Airbnb can earn you a weekly average of what one can earn in their area. If you are providing extra amenities like meals and extra beds, you can earn extra cash too. Airbnb also offers a smart pricing feature which allows the price of your listing to increase or decrease based on the general demand for listings like the property you are offering.

Peer to Peer Lending

Peer to peer lending allows you to lend money to people who don't qualify for traditional financing. This is not only simple, but also a great way to earn decent interest on your money. Of course, you might have to be slightly careful about who you are lending your hard-earned money to, but you can always play it safe by doing a little background search on the person who is borrowing, or simply chose to lend money to your friends or family.

How do you get started? Typically, you might have to invest in several small loans so, instead of risking your money by investing in one big loan, which makes it extremely risky, you won't lose a lot of money by investing in numerous small loans. For instance, if you have $2,000 for the investment, then you can offer 10 loans worth $200 each. How much can you earn? Let me warn you that this business idea involves a certain amount of risk, and it's certainly not for the faint of heart. That said, it is highly-rewarding. You will typically see a return between 5% and 9%, which is much greater when compared to other ways of generating interest.

Design and Sell Your Own Merchandise

Tees, tops, mugs, pens or photo frames – you can design just about anything and sell it online. If your designing skills are decent, you can create and display your own merchandise on various platforms on the Internet. All you need to do is come with an original design, customize it, and then put it up for sale to earn some money. Of course, you need to have basic artistic skills to be able to design your merchandise, but you certainly needn't be an expert. You can also take the help of programs such as Adobe Illustrator to better your creations.

How do you get started? You can set up your own website, and start generating as much traffic as you can so people can view your creations. How much can you earn? This is a difficult question to answer as your earning will totally depend upon how unique and how much in demand your merchandise is. That being said, you can charge a slightly higher price for your products once your website starts getting more traffic.

Browse the Internet

Not a lot of people believe me when I tell them that they can actually make money by simply browsing the Internet. There are companies out there who are ready to pay you money to browse the Internet. This, of course, is different from other passive income ideas in the list like stock photos or writing books where you can get paid upfront as soon as you put in the work. Here, companies will pay you to search some specific items on the Internet. Websites like Swagbucks, Inbox dollars, Microsoft rewards, etc. allow you to earn either cash or points that you can exchange for vouchers.

How much can you earn? This option of earning passive income is not going to make you rich overnight or even earn you the same money as some of the options mentioned above, but it can help you earn some cash without doing much. Most of us are browsing the Internet throughout the day anyway – for online shopping, watching movies, glancing through people's social media profiles etc.

Create an Online Course

If you have enough knowledge about a specific topic, such as gardening, pottery, jewelry, organic cooking, WordPress etc., you should consider creating your own online course and selling it online. There are several websites that will allow you to create an online course about a particular topic and help you sell it. The courses can consist of videos, articles, or even videos. How do you get started? For starters, crate a course around your topic of expertise. You don't necessarily have to make your own website to sell the course. There is a plethora of online learning platforms that bring together people who wish to teach and the ones who want to learn. All you have to do is upload your online course, and soon you will have users looking to purchase your course.

How much money can you make? There are some people who are making a full-time income by selling their online courses on sites like Teachable and Udemy. How much you earn will totally depend upon the quality of the course, how much you decide to sell it for, and the commission charged by the website you are using, etc. That said, there are several people who have been making a huge amount of money through these online courses.

Create a YouTube Channel

Isn't this the most fun job? If you don't like blog writing, then you should consider setting up your own YouTube channel. Each time a viewer views an ad in your videos, you earn money. This requires you to become a YouTube partner. How do you get started? Absolutely anyone can start a YouTube channel. If you don't already have a Google account, you will have to sign up for one. Once you do, then you can sign up for your YouTube channel. Making money by uploading videos sounds very easy, but don't be delusional and think that you can make a huge sum of money right from the outset. You will have to upload videos with great content and be consistent with it. When you consistently strive to offer the best content to your subscriber, you will soon start making some decent money. You can also earn commission by becoming a YouTube partner to earn some commission from Google AdSense.

How much will you earn? Although I can't tell you exactly how much you can make, as per the general estimate, YouTubers earn around $0.25 - $7 per 1,000 views. If you look up on the Internet, you will come across tons of success stories of people who earn a full-time income through their YouTube channels.

Open a High-Yielding Savings Account

We know how important a saving account can be, especially in times of emergencies. Luckily enough, due to online banks, there are tons of savings accounts that offer better interest rates to the borrowers. Opening a high-yielding savings account is a less risky, yet profitable way of making money. How do you get started? You will need to open a savings account with any of these banks, deposit some money in the account and sit back as you start drawing the interest money. If you don't like to go through the hassle of investing, then having a high-yielding savings account is a great alternative.

How much can you earn? Needless to say, the amount of interest you will earn depends upon the amount of money you deposit. The higher the deposit, the higher will be your earnings. FNBO offers a user-friendly calculator, which can help you get a fair idea of how much you can earn. As per the calculator, if someone deposits an amount of $5,000, he or she will earn about $65 in interest during the first year of savings.

Get Paid to Advertise on Your Car

As per a study conducted by the AAA Foundation of Traffic Safety, most Americans spend an average of 293 hours driving every year. Think about it...wouldn't it be nice to get paid for the same amount of time you invest in driving the car? For that, you will have to be willing to place some advertisements on your car to make yourself some money. It's one of the easiest ways of making some passive income. How do you get started? There are a lot of companies in the market which will pay you a good amount of cash for sticking advertisements on your car. You will have to reach out to one of these companies, such as FreeCarMedia or Wrapify, and let them know that you are open to wrap your car with advertisements.

How much can you earn? One of the most important factors that affect your earning from advertisements is your location. For instance, if most of your driving happens in a populated city, then you will earn more as compared to someone who stays in a quiet suburb. As per Wrapify, if you drive in a place like San Diego, you could make up to $300 a month. There are several drivers out there who are earning about $450 every month just by wrapping advertisements around their cars.

Buy a Website (Existing)

You can certainly earn from building your own blog, but if you do not have the time and patience required to build a successful blog, then you can consider using an existing website. One of the best things about these websites is that they can offer you a consistent income. How do you get started? You can log on to a website called Flippa which specializes in selling and buying websites. Flippa is nothing but an online market platform, which allows you to purchase existing websites. You can easily pick from the plethora of websites here belonging to different niches, from food and fashion to careers. Most of these listings also offer information on the specific income that these sites make every month.

How much do you earn? Having your own website can be highly profitable, but you need to do a little market research before buying one. If you pick the right website, you may earn somewhere between $1,000 - $4,000 each month on Flippa. For more information on Flippa, log on to their website to get a fair idea of the average earning you can make each month.

Become a FBA Seller

Designing your own merchandise, writing your own book, or creating a blog sounds interesting, but what if you don't have a creative bone in your body? You can purchase stuff like DVD's, clothes or jewelry and start selling it on your own website. You can sell these items even when you don't have your own website, but you will still need to use your convincing skills to get people to buy your stuff. For these reasons, selling your stuff via Amazon is a better idea. Amazon runs a program known as the Fulfillment by Amazon (FBA), which helps you to sell your products while taking responsibility for everything else right from customer service to shipping. Amazon is also one of the most trusted retailers to increase your sales.

How do you get started? Crate an Amazon Seller Account and later add FBA to the account. The next step is to create listings for the items you are planning to sell and then add your products to their catalogue. Once you finish this step, you can integrate the inventory-management software using the Amazon API. How much can you earn? Your earning will depend on the profit margins. Also, keep in mind that Amazon charges fulfillment fees, so price your products accordingly.

Sign up for Reward Programs

Several restaurants, brands, stores, and many other retailers who wish to keep their consumers happy come up with reward programs for them. These programs offer you rewards, such as cash back or discounts in the form of coupons or credit cards. How do you get started? There are several reward programs that you can sign up for, including Petco Pals Rewards, CVS extracare, OfficeMax rewards/ Office depot and many others.

How much can you earn? This income opportunity won't draw you huge money like becoming an FBA seller, selling apps or courses; however, it does offer you an opportunity to earn some extra cash while you are trying to set up your main gig. Each restaurant or store will offer you their own rewards depending upon the part of the reward program you are a part of. For instance, if you are a part of a reward program with Petco Pals, it offers 5% cash back on purchases, while a company like CVS Extracare may offer a certain percentage of cash back.

Sell Your Music

If you happen to be musically inclined, then selling your music is a great way of making money using your unique talent. Just like stock photos, one can license their music and earn some royalty money from it. There are thousands of people looking to add some great music to their videos; for instance, a YouTuber who wishes to add some original music to his or her YouTube videos might want to purchase your music. Of course, this is going to take some effort initially, but once you create a unique piece of music and put it up for sale, you will find a lot of people asking to buy it. What more, you can also keep earning from the same track over and over again.

How do get started? You can sign up on websites like Pond5, Productiontrax, AudioJungle and PremiumBeat etc. How much can you earn? Your income will depend on a few factors, such as:

- The number of sales you make;

- The price you sell your tracks for; and

- The amount of commission you get.

A website like Pond5 might offer you a 50% commission, while The Music Case can offer you a 43% commission.

As per The Guardian, certain musicians are making about $30,000 - $40,000 every year by selling their music online.

Start Affiliate Marketing

Affiliating marketing is getting popular day by day, and if you haven't considered this option of making money, then its high time you should. If you are particularly looking for a more hands-off way of making money, then you should consider selling someone else's products on your own website. This process is called affiliate marketing. Also, you don't necessarily have to have a blog to do affiliate marketing. Once you become an affiliate marketer, you get a product link for selling. Every time a person buys a product using your product link, you get a commission. This commission can range between 1% and 75%, or sometimes even more. You can chose to promote your affiliate links using several ways such as blog posts, social media posts, comparison review sites, or product resources page.

How do you get started you ask, well, by finding products to promote, and the easiest ways to do this is by signing up for an affiliate program from networks such as Amazon Associates, ShareASale, Rakuten Marketing or even clickbank. How much can you earn? You can start earning from $5 as a beginner and up to $1,000,000 per month once you become an established marketer.

Buy a Vending Machine

This is a great start-up idea for people who are short on their business capital. It's not only a low-maintenance business idea, but it also doesn't require much effort on your part. All you may need to do is re-stock the vending machine every now and then, but except that part, you literally don't have to do anything. How do you get started? For starters, you will need to buy a vending machine. This machine can be bought online or through a vending machine franchise shop in your area. If you are a newbie, you will need to buy a vending machine and also source the locations yourself. For that, you will need to do a little market research with regards to the area where the demand for such machines is high. Typically, these areas include malls, schools, movie halls, and even airports. Once you decide on what type of food you wish to offer, such as bagels, sandwiches, candies, or health foods, you can start making money.

How much can you earn? Your income may depend upon various factors like:

- The number of sales you get

- The type of products you sell

- Your profit margin

- The location in which the vending machine is placed

Another thing that you have to keep in mind is that you may have to compensate the property owner for allowing you to install the machine in his or her premises. You also have to pay them a commission which can range anywhere between 10 - 20%.

Turn Your Existing Business into a Source of Passive Income

If you have a business which is up and running, but, for some reason, it's taking up a lot of your time, then you can consider outsourcing it. This will instantly turn your business into a great source of earning some passive income. Having a successful business can be immensely satisfying and profitable, but the everyday stresses can take a toll on your health. That's why you might want to consider outsourcing your business. On the other hand, if you don't already have a business, but you wish to start one, then you can also try outsourcing a lot of start-up work too.

How do you get started? You can find people to help you run your business on websites such as Guru, Freelancer, Upwork, Fiverr or PeoplePerHour. How much can you earn? Most people who have outsourced their work through these websites have managed to earn $1,000 out of the business, which they had initially started for $100 for less.

Become a Silent Business Partner

Don't want to go through the hassle of running a business? You can simply become a silent business partner. A silent business partner doesn't have to put any effort in running or outsourcing the business except investing money in the business. A silent partner isn't involved in any of the daily business operations or business meetings either. How do you get started? If you have enough money to invest in a business, then you can look for companies who are looking for monetary help to start their business. You can also invest your money in an existing business and help them run it better. Just make sure that you do a little market research before investing your money as being a silent business partner doesn't mean that it doesn't have any risk. After all, who wants to lose their hard-earned money? How much can you earn? As much as the business makes, so ensure that you chose a profitable business to invest in.

Use a Credit Card or Cashback

Imagine getting back a certain percentage of your money back every time you spend it on a purchase? Well, credit cards can make that happen for you. There are several credit cards that offer their customers some decent cashback amount on their purchases. While some of the credit card companies give you cashback on every single purchase, the others will offer you cashback at specific outlets, such as the departmental store, grocery store or gas stations. So, get to know exactly what the credit card company is offering you in terms of cashback while signing up for one.

How do you get started? You can consider signing up for various credit cards such as American Express Blue Cash Preferred Card, Capital One Quicksilver card, Citi Double Cash Card and many more. How much can you earn? As per a report published by the USDA, on average every person spends about $200 - $300 on monthly groceries but, lets' say you stay in a two-person household and your monthly expenses are $600. If you purchase them via a credit card that offers you 5% cashback, then your cashback amount will be $30. While this may not seem like a huge amount, if you keep earning this amount on every purchase, soon it will add up to $100 every year.

Invest with a Robo-Advisor

With a Robo-advisor, you can let an algorithm manage all your investments, and this is as passive as you get. What is a Robo-advisor? Robo-advisors are nothing but digital platforms that use algorithm-driven technology to make high-investment quality available to each one of us. If you have some money to start with, you can invest with one of the largest Robo-advisors in the market known as Betterment. There's absolutely no minimum amount that you need to invest; in fact, the fees are quite low (generally between 0.25% - 0.4%); plus, you don't really have to be an expert investor. How do you get started? Here's how:

- Sign up for an account without any minimum deposit.

- Describe yourself on Betterment. For instance, why are you investing? Where do you stand in your financial life? Are you looking to earn some money for a vacation?

- Depending upon your answers to such questions, Betterment will then suggest an appropriate investment plan for you using their advanced technology.

You can also opt for Blooom, which works in the same way Betterment does, but only for your 401k plan. Blooom also offers a free analysis of your current retirement plan sponsored by your employer.

Rent out Your Car, Parking Space or Bike

Got a car, parking space, or a bike? You should seriously think about renting it out for some cash. Similar to renting out a property, renting your car or bike may require some maintenance work, but it is certainly worth the money you earn from it. How do you get started? If you wish to rent out your car while you are on a holiday, you can sign up on websites such as Splinlister and Turo. If you register with Turo, you are offered a $1 million protection in liability insurance while your car is covered against physical damage or theft of any kind. Registration on Splinlister is free of charge, but they will charge you about 17.5% as a commission fee for every rental. This website also covers the safety of your vehicle up to $10,000.

Similarly, if you have a free parking space, a garage or a driveway, you can simply list it on Craigslist. How much can you earn? That depends upon the locality in which you stay. For instance, if you reside in a popular metropolitan area, you will be gladly surprised at the kind of money you will get.

Start Your Online Store

Building your online store is easier than you think. If you wish to start your own business, but don't have enough capital to start one, then this option is ideal for you. There is a plethora of business models available for e-commerce websites.

- You can sell a physical product: This may require some amount of capital to start with, but you can sell some unique products to make maximum profit out of your investment.

- Sell your own digital products: Again, this may require some work and money, but you don't have to worry about the products getting delivered.

- Dropshipping: The best part about dropshipping is that you don't have to own the stock. Once you sell a product from your online store, the manufacturer will directly ship the product to the consumer.

How much will you earn? It depends upon the pricing of your product and the amount of traffic you generate towards your website. There are so many people out there who are making huge profits by selling products online.

Sell Printables on Autopilot

If you love art, then you can easily sell digital products on Etsy as a way of earning yourself some passive income. Digital products don't require a lot of maintenance; plus, your customers will receive a direct link to download them, and that means you will not have to worry about the shipping as well as the returns handling. You can simply spend your quality time creating some beautiful artwork.

Some of the most printable items are as following:

- Wall art

- Home decorations

- Greeting cards

- Invitations

- Organizer

There is no limit to your imagination; you can create several different printables at the same time. Can you cook? Are you good at organizing? Can you make a meal plan, or a weight-loss diet plan? Great, you can use your expertise to make some wonderful printables. As long as your work hits a chord with the audience and is of top-notch quality, it will always find buyers. How much can you earn? If you sell your printables on platforms such as Amazon, you may get just about 30% of the original price; whereas, if you sell them on your own website, you will certainly make a good amount of money since you don't have to pay commission.

Subscription or Membership Fees

A great way to generate some income through your creative work or writing skills is to sell it using a membership site. Through the membership sites, visitors will pay you membership fees or subscription fees to access your content, which may include videos, courses, articles, lectures, or anything that people will be willing to pay for. How do you get started? You can sell your stuff through websites such as Blog Mastermind, which aims at teaching people how to make money via online blogging. Since more and more people are willing to pay for such content, you can write some useful articles on this website and sell them. As soon as you start selling your content, you will start earning money through the membership fees they pay.

How much can you earn? To make more money on a membership site, you need to keep uploading fresh content regularly so that the existing customers can keep renewing their membership, thereby allowing you to earn some cash through membership fees.

Create a Lead Generation Website

What is a lead generation website? A lead generation website is created to provide referrals to local businesses. For instance, if you create your own lead generation website which focuses mainly on health and fitness, then you would want to educate people about healthy foods, lifestyle habits that need to be corrected, and exercises etc. Within the website, you can provide links for your viewers to contact you, and once they do, you can refer them to health professionals or dieticians in your area. These professionals will then pay you a commission for generating them a lead.

How do you get started? Start building a website around a particular niche and then work on generating as much traffic as you can so more and more people can contact you. You can simply sign up on WordPress.com for creating your website, buy a domain name and then get started. How much can you earn? It depends upon the commission you get from the clients you refer. You can also make a decent amount of money by getting advertisers on your website. Remember, the key to your success is to get your website on top of all the search engine pages.

Invest in Office Space

Virtually or literally, it's the same thing as a rental property investment. The only difference is that instead of renting out the space to families, you are renting it out to an office. One of the most popular trends using this idea is to reconstruct an old building and rent it out for a commercial space. Renovated office space is becoming a popular way of earning some passive income all across the country. Almost everyone wants to invest their money in an old building with huge spaces inside.

How do you get started? Well, to start with, this option does require you to put in a huge chunk of cash, so if you don't have that kind of money, you can skip this idea. On the other hand, if you do have some savings, and you decide to invest it in an office space, you will be making huge profits within a short period of time. You would only need to look after the maintenance of the property at regular intervals, along with some paper work.

Create Software

Are you a tech buff? If you are, then the chances are that you are capable of creating software. Just like a phone app creation, building software can be done online. If you have some amount of programming experience, then you can certainly create your own app, but if you don't then you can simply hire a programmer through websites such as Upwork, Fiverr, or Freelancer and get an app created.

How to pick a niche and get started? Contact your nearby mortar or brick business owners to find out what kind of problems they generally face. For instance, if you call the nearby dry cleaning store and you notice that they are all facing one particular problem, then you can come up with software that fixes it.

You can call the same business owners and tell them that you have a solution for their problems, and tell them that you can give them a discount on your app if they pay you upfront. How much money can you make? If you are able to nail a specific problem and offer appropriate solutions through your app, you will have business owners throwing money at your feet. Now, income generation through this idea will take you a lot of research, time and patience, but it's worth all the efforts once your app starts selling.

Create a Comparison Site

Most people including me, when they are trying to choose between two products to buy, the very first thing that they do is compare them. There are several comparison websites that educate you about the good and bad points about a particular product, which makes it easier for you to buy it as per your priority. Take a pair of shoes for instance. If I am trying to pick between Nike Pegasus and Adidas Boost, the first thing I am going to do is Google them to find out as much information as I can. This is where a comparison website comes in the picture. It helps you chose the right product considering the consumer's needs. You can add some affiliate links on your comparison website, so every time a consumer buys a particular product using your affiliate link, you get a cut from the sale. How much can you make? The more comparison you do, the more traffic you generate, and the higher are your chances of making money.

Airmiles Credit Card

Airmiles are not acknowledged for the goldmine they are. When you sign up for an Airmiles card, you get huge sign-up bonuses. Also, it is one of the easiest and the most convenient ways of getting some free travel. Most people don't sign up for an Airmiles card owing to the high annual fees, but you can always put it on your credit card and churn that. Plus, applying for several credit cards at the same time doesn't really do any damage to your credit score. So why not take a chance? All you have to do is ensure that you are not late on your payments that often lead to huge interest.

How do you get started? No prizes for guessing - you will have to simply apply for an Airmiles credit card. How much do you earn? There are certain cards which offer about 150,000 as bonus points which can be converted into $1,500. This is one of the smartest ways of earning yourself some residual income. Remember, you can't go on a shopping spree using this credit card, always use it wisely and don't forget to pay the card on time.

Online Garage Sale

Are you looking to get rid of some of your stuff? Why not make a few bucks out of it? Garage sales are one of the most loved passive income ideas, although your main goal would be to clean your house. It's not surprising that more and more people are having garage sales, considering the kind of money one can make without having to invest anything. If you do find something for cheap which you think can attract buyers, you can sell it for a lightly higher price on websites like eBay and earn a healthy profit. How do you get started? You can either create your own website or sign up on websites like eBay and put up pictures of the product you wish to sell and take it from there on.

How much can you earn out of it? If you are selling something which you already own, you will be making 100% profit, whereas, even if you buy something for cheap and sell it online, you will still be making a good amount of profit. It may take some time for you to figure out how to determine which stuff is junk and the one you can re-sell, but it's not rocket science.

Party Chair and Rental Table

Events like birthdays, anniversaries or weddings can sometimes cost a fortune. The surprising part is that most people have no qualms about paying a fortune either. Part of the big expense includes renting chairs and tables for the ceremony. If you have a huge house or some storage space, you can buy some tables and chairs, click pictures of the new tables and chairs, and start marketing them to viewers. This can be done through your own website or through other rental websites. People are always looking for renting products for a lesser price, and your website could present a perfect opportunity for them.

Try to take some time out to assess the cost of fancy looking chairs, where you can get them for a lesser price and then decide the price accordingly. How much can you earn? If you are renting out tables and chairs for a big wedding, then you are up for some huge cash flow. Birthdays, anniversaries or house-warming parties may not earn you much, but they are still a good way earning yourself some passive income.

Start a Fitness Gym

No, it doesn't have to be a fancy-looking gym with 40 ellipticals and 30 treadmills. You can simply look for an open space or a huge room in your neighborhood and rent it. Thereafter, you will have to buy some basic gym equipment like dumbbells, barbells, kettle bells, a treadmill or a stationary bike for starters. The next step is to find some customers. How do you do that? By marketing your gym. When it comes to gyms, most people are looking for a hygienic gym that is located as close to their house as possible, so make sure that you aggressively market yourself, especially around your neighborhood.

How much can you earn? If you get more customers, then your chances of earning a whopping amount of cash is high. Keep in mind that you will also have to pay rent to the property owner, the gym trainers, and pay for the electricity bills too. Also, you will be responsible for maintaining the equipment installed in the gym. Nevertheless, it's a great way of earning yourself some passive income, especially if you are a fitness enthusiast yourself.

SEO Consulting for Local Businesses

Today, people only go searching for a product in the real world if they don't get it in the digital world. For instance, if I were to buy a frame, I will quickly start looking for frame stores online. I am going to find out reviews about the product to help me decide which one is better. When it comes to local businesses, they need some help to stand out. If you start ranking higher for a local search, then you are certainly going to get more business.

How do you get started? If you have some knowledge about SEO, or at least have a bit of desire to learn, then you can earn yourself a decent income. You don't have to be a subject matter expert, but you should certainly know more than the storeowners. Tell them what you can do for them and how you can help them grow their business. This will not only help their local rankings, but earn you a good amount of cash too.

Party Hall Rental

This is certainly a competitive business, especially when it comes to wedding venue rentals. Couples struggle to find a venue for their impending ceremony and book them months, or even a year in advance. All the venue owner has to do is get the word out, and soon people start calling him or her for bookings. Unlike renting your house, this one doesn't require a lot of maintenance. How do you get started? Start looking for the perfect venue. Imagine if you were getting married, what type of venue would you like? Something fun or exciting? Exactly! Pick a venue that is spacious enough to host an entertaining party. Strike a deal with the property owner and start marketing it using social media platforms.

Some of these properties might require a bit of work. Also, you will have to invest a large chunk of cash at the start, but, after the initial investment, you can simply sit back and relax while the property earns you a good amount of passive residual income.

Build a Social Media Following

Most people don't believe me when I tell them that they can earn themselves a passive income just by building their social media following. Making some money from your social media account may seem like an impossible dream for many, but in reality, it's quite simple. There are a lot of people who are gaining fame by collaborating with a few other creators in order to build Social Bluebook. What is Social Bluebook? Social Bluebook tells you how much your social media net is worth if you enter the total number of followers you have on Instagram, Twitter, and Facebook, etc.

How much can you earn? As soon as your followers start increasing, you might have a few companies approach you in order to promote their brand. Some of them will even help you strike a deal with an advertiser. All you need to do is gather as much following as possible to gain more traffic, and eventually help you gain a significant amount of money. Making money by merely uploading a few pictures on my Instagram, Facebook, and Twitter accounts, etc. sounds pretty good to me.

White Labeling

What is white labeling? It means that you would be branding a product created by someone else. One of the most commonly white-labeled products are supplements and vitamins. Take, for instance, someone like Nuticap labs from where you generally order fish oil, vitamin C or other such supplements. Of course, the pill formula will be theirs, but you will be the one who will brand and market it the way you like and the way you think it will garner more attention. How do you get started? Start with branding an undeserved product or look for a product which is lagging behind on an important demographic and start marketing it.

One trick would be to sell good quality multivitamins to youngsters, but make sure to be ethical while promoting a product to teenagers. Do not, and I repeat, do not, market a product whose quality you are unsure of. Most people in their 20s do not consider taking multivitamin pills even when they are suffering from vitamin deficiencies, so you can design a marketing strategy that will appeal to them. How much can you make? Once you create your own website on Shopify and start selling the products, you could earn a good amount of cash.

Set up a Coupon Website

Do you like a good bargain? Well, who doesn't? Have you ever stumbled on a coupon website and wondered how it makes money? Did you know that the coupon industry is the most powerful influencer of customer purchase decisions in the country? Most people don't spend too much time on a coupon website; they just grab the code they need and get off the site. Once you put in the coupon code, a cookie is automatically placed in your browser, allowing the merchant to check whether you were referred by an affiliate. Each time you buy something, the coupon site is paid a commission. Unlike other websites, coupon websites do not need a lot of content, and this is a good thing if you don't like writing.

Do you have a niche in mind? Then start building your website using Bluehost and WordPress. How much can you earn? The major portion of your income is going to be through affiliate links. The amount of money you will earn through affiliate marketing will depend upon website-to-website.

Be an Online Coach

If you specialize in a particular field, you can coach people online and make some money. Posing yourself as an expert in a specific area can get you tons of people wanting to pay you for your time. Being an online coach doesn't need any initial investment either. All you have to do is sign up on platforms such as Coach.me, Savvy.is and Clarity.fm etc. and get started. If you can successfully package your experience, as well as coaching skills, into an easy-to-learn program, you will be earning a significant amount of income each month.

How much can you earn? Since you can only charge for the time you offer, it can seem like a limited passive income option, but there are thousands of coaches making a good amount of money for their online coaching packages. This is also one of the quickest ways of setting up a passive income business online without investing any money at all.

Share Your Stories through Podcasts

Podcast are hot right now. Considering how busy our lives have become, podcasting is a great opportunity to grab the attention of your audience within a short span while making some money. In fact, Josh Lee Dumas earns over $200,000 each month from interviewing entrepreneurs every single day in his podcast 'Entrepreneur on Fire'. What do you have to do to get started? You need to come up with interesting content that will engage the audience and start building your following. Take some time out to decide on a particular topic that you would like to make a podcast about, and then start recording your voice. There are many companies such as Blue, Behnringer, Focusrite and many others which sell top-notch quality plug and play podcast set-ups which can help you get your recording today.

How much can you earn? To earn money from your podcasts, you will have to have a strategy to monetize the podcast. Start with a basic website to share your episodes and thereafter monetize it using the following options:

- Live shows

- Sell your own products

- Crowdfunding and donations

- Sell subscriber-only content

- Traditional advertising

All of the above options will help you gain a significant amount of money each month.

Narrate Audiobooks

Yes, you can make money by simply reading audiobooks. The audiobook industry is trending right now, but only about 5% of the books are getting converted into audio format. If you have some voice modulation skills and have a clear diction, or you have always been complimented on your voice, then you should seriously consider recording audio version of popular books. There are various sites, such as ACX, that helps to connect the authors with the audiobook recorders.

How do you get started? The best way to market your skills is by uploading your voice samples on your website and then approach websites like ACX. How much can you earn? That entirely depends upon what the current market pay is, and how much the author is ready to pay. Nevertheless, you will be making yourself a decent amount of money by recording for audiobooks.

Sign up for Medium's Partner Program

Medium is a community that allows you to post essays or articles and showcases your work in front of millions of readers every month. It's actually a great place for someone who wishes to build an audience for his or her blog or stumble upon customers for their consulting business. Besides that, you can also use Medium's new partner program to make money whenever anyone reads your articles. How do you get started? The registration is absolutely free of cost and you can decide whether you wish to make your articles freely available to people, or exclusively readable for people who pay $5 for a premium membership with Medium.

How much can you earn? The amount of money you shall make will be based on how many people engage with your posts on a monthly basis. If you are willing to consistently write great pieces worth reading, then you can earn between $500 - $1,500 each month. In fact, if you keep up with your posts, you can even find the potential to make thousands of dollars each month.

Help People with Their Taxes

This is not one of those glorious online passive income ideas, but it can certainly get you a fair amount of money. After all, everyone needs help when it comes to filing for their taxes. Almost every individual or business requires someone to help them prepare their tax returns, and this is where you come into the picture. You should start by targeting resources or time-strapped small business owners. If you are interested in getting certified, you can enroll yourself with the income tax school, which offers a wide variety of training programs that can certify you as a tax consultant within 10 weeks.

How much can you earn? Once the tax season starts rolling in, you can charge an average of $229 per case as a freelance tax consultant as per the reports by CNBC.

Transcribe Audios and Interviews

Almost everyone from journalists to lawyers, to doctors, or researchers need to record their interviews every day. Not just that, but they also require someone who can transcribe their interviews. If you like listening to audios and don't mind playing them over and over again while you pen down all the information, then there's a good chance that you can make some money online transcribing audios for people.

How much can you earn? Most services are ready to pay their transcribers anywhere between $15 - $25 for every single hour of the transcribed audio. If you specialize in medical transcription, you can earn even more money. If you are a newbie who's interested in medical transcription, then you can log on to platforms such as Quicktate, Transcribeme, Transcribe Anywhere, Tigerfish, Rev and Crowdsurf.

Proofread Articles

As long as humans write, there will always be requirement for editors. Proofreading or freelance editing offers you a chance of earning a decent pay while also encouraging you to read about all sorts of interesting topics. What's more, if you are interested in pursuing a career as a full-time editor, it can allow you to live a life completely on your terms. You can even travel across the globe as a digital nomad. How do you get started? Simply sign up on freelance websites such as Upwork, Fiver, or Freelancer and start looking for clients who need help with editing.

How much can you make? If your editing skills have reached a level where you can be called an expert, then you will be earning yourself a huge amount of cash per client but, even if you are a newbie, you can make a decent amount of earning within the first couple of months itself.

Online Travel Consultant

If you like to travel, then one of the easiest ways of earning yourself some passive income is to turn into a private travel agent. One of my friends did just that and now he is making a good amount of money through his travel consulting business. How do you get started? I recommend that you begin with word of mouth recommendations from the people you know so they contact you each time they travel. Later, you can also create an online social media profile for yourself on LinkedIn or Facebook and invite people to keep up with the latest deals.

How much money can you make? On average, you can make anywhere between $500 - $5,000 USD once your business takes off. As you progress, you can find yourself earning more and more cash.

Enter Contests for Slogans and Company Names

How witty are your one-liners? Did you have a dream of entering the field of advertising, but couldn't? Here's your chance to put all your skills to use by writing slogans or through company naming. There are lots of opportunities for people who can come up with catchy slogans. For those who have a knack for names, they can sign up on squadhelp.com or nameforce.com.

How much can you earn? If you sign up on slogan writing sites like Sloganslingers.com, then the prize money ranges between $200 to $999 and the money will be transferred to your account within 24 - 48 hours.

Get Paid to Stay Fit

You won't earn a lot of money by using this option, but it's a great gig if you are someone who is already working towards staying fit. There are several apps in the market, such as AchieveMint, which can reward you for walking, counting your calorie intake, or by asking you to take health surveys. How does AchieveMint work? It is operated by connecting to different fitness apps that you might already be accessing, such as Healthkit, Runkeeper, Fitbit and MyFitnessPal, while allowing you points for specific interactions.

How much can you earn? On average, one can earn around $10 per 10,000 points without putting any limitation on their earnings.

Write Reviews of the Places You have been to

Do you like giving feedback every time you buy a product? How often do you look up a restaurant review before visiting it? Most of our world is run on reviews; so how about making some money by writing reviews online? How do you get started? You can create accounts on websites like Software Judge, FameBit and Vindale research, Influence Central, CrowdTap and Modern Mom, but don't just jump your guns and start writing reviews before you read their terms and conditions.

How much can you earn? Now, this isn't a guaranteed source of earning a huge income, but it's definitely worth it. You just need to ensure that you are writing reviews on websites that are good paying and worth your time.

Become a Columnist or Online News Writer

No, you don't require a degree in journalism to be able to earn yourself a passive income as a columnist or online reporter. If you have always aspired to be a journalist but don't have the formal education to do so, this is your golden chance. Of course, you need good writing skills and clear perspectives, but this passive income idea will not only earn you a good income, but also give you a chance to put your skills to good use. There are so many websites that can function better with some help on acquiring local coverage.

How do you get started? Start approaching these news websites and let them know that you wish to work with them. The best thing to do would be to start your own website and upload some crisp articles on it so you can use them as samples when you start pitching to the websites. How much can you earn? The pay differs from website-to-website, but a site like The Examiner offers a good amount of compensation for the contributors as per the ad revenue generated by the article.

Data Analysis for Companies

Do you like working with numbers? If so, this passive income idea is ideal for you. Several companies are always on the lookout for talented contractors who are experts in data analysis that makes this option one of the most lucrative ways of making money online. If you have some expertise or credentials related to this field, you can get started right away by logging on to platforms such as Digiserved and Upwork.

How much can you earn? The amount of money you make will completely depend on the current market rates.

Online Fitness Coach

If you are a fitness enthusiast, have the charisma of becoming a coach, along with a bit of business sense, you can become a part-time fitness trainer for people online. Being a personal fitness trainer is not only monetarily rewarding, but it's also helpful in keeping yourself motivated to stay fit. How do you get started? You can start a fitness blog and then start looking out for clients through social media and other fitness websites.

How much can you earn? Once you establish a reputation of being a dedicated fitness trainer, you will be easily able to turn this thing into a full-time endeavor if you wish. If you search the Internet, there are several fitness bloggers making a good amount of income for themselves.

Create DIY Videos

If you have the knack for creating stuff from scratch, you can start your own online DIY channel. Believe it or not, most people are constantly looking for stuff that can be created without spending a whole lot of money, and you can help them do just that. Pick out a niche you would like to create DIY videos about, sign up on YouTube or start your own website and start generating some great content.

How do you get started? Sign up on websites like DarbySmart or Barkbox and Mattel, upload your content and start monetizing the videos using views and ads. How much can you earn? If your content is unique and you can offer a whole load of value to the viewers, then you can expect a good amount of income each month.

Edit Videos Online

Visual media is growing like crazy, especially videos. There are a lot of people out there looking for some expert help to edit their raw footage to make it into viral-worth content. If you have some software knowledge and have worked with videos, then you can make some money as an online editor. What do you have to do for it? Simply sign up on websites like ProductionHub, Creative Cow Job Search and many others and look out for clients.

How much can you earn? Once you start getting multiple clients, on an average, you can earn about $28 per hour or more.

Become a Customer Service Support Online

Do you like talking to people or helping them out with their issues? If so, you should consider working as a customer service support superstar for various companies across the globe. Considering that this job requires 24/7 help, there are many companies who are always on the lookout for someone in different time zones to help them out with the problems their users are facing.

How do you get started? Sign up on platforms like Upwork or Fiverr and contact the clients who need some customer service help. How much can you earn? That depends upon company to company, but you can start off with $10 per hour and then gradually earn more.

CHAPTER TWO

30-Day Passive Income Challenge

Now, I don't want you to count an exact 30-day period and use it as a measure for your success. Chances are that you may need a little more or less than 30 days to get the ball rolling. That said, this 30-day challenge is sure to put you on the right track to start earning money through the passive income ideas mentioned in this book. I have broken down the challenge into 4 weeks and here are the steps you need to act on:

Week One

Manage your time like a Ninja. Like, seriously! You would need to figure out a way to allot some time to work on the passive income stream you are going to pick, so, all that Netflix binge watching needs to STOP right now.

Once you allot yourself a time slot, think about all the topics you seem to be interested in. An even better option would be to list down your skills on a piece of paper and then pick a topic that can help you blend your interests and passion together.

Get invested in learning as much as you can about the topic at hand. For instance, if you have decided to earn money using your teaching skills or blog writing, then search for articles which teach you how to blog or how to go ahead about conducting an online class.

Week Two

If your primary day job takes up most of your time, then you need to start outsourcing some of your work. It could mean getting yourself a housekeeper or hiring a virtual assistant for a few hours per week. Some of us are worried that we won't be able to afford it because what if we don't manage to rope in enough work? This thinking may sound uncertain certainly hilarious, but don't let it stop you from getting some outside help. Once you start offloading, you will find it easier to work on your projects better, make more money and, in turn, pay these assistants well.

Week Three

Don't just keep throwing articles, blog posts or reviews like factory-churned products that come out of the same mold some spaghetti on the wall. Don't let your work be a chore, and ensure that you truly enjoy what you are doing. Only pick niches that are easy and fun to work on, and always listen to your audience. If what you are offering doesn't seem up to the mark, be ready to make the necessary adjustments.

Once you are clear on what you want to do, start selling stuff right away rather than spending days pondering over which idea is more monetizing. No matter which niche you pick, know that sooner or later you will be able to earn money from it.

Week Four

Once your website is up, or your profile on websites like Amazon, Upwork, Fiverr, or others seems to have enough content, start making use of your social media connections as much as possible. That said; don't underestimate the benefit of mouth publicity. Be ready to talk about what you do and invite your friends and family to check out your work.

Be ready to rinse and repeat. Don't ditch the idea of exploring a new territory. For instance, when I first started off, I didn't have a blog and directly jumped on to making some DIY YouTube videos. I then realized that my followers were not increasing, so I went back to the basics and built a blog over time and that helped me increase the number of followers on my channel.

Lastly, don't lose heart if something doesn't work, and don't hesitate to change the niche, but, you should only think about changing niches once you have exhausted all your efforts and still feel like the income isn't matching your expectations.

Here's the thing about passive income; there's absolutely nothing passive when it comes to the creation phase of your product. It requires some serious hustle on your part for the first few weeks, but, once the initial work is done, you can expect some leveraged income coming your way.

Conclusion

I wish to thank you all once again for purchasing this book and for taking the time out to consider the possibility of earning passive income. I agree, it's Utopian by design, but if you think that earning yourself some extra money isn't possible because of your day job, then it's time to think again. It's not only possible to generate passive income, but it would be absolutely silly of people to not put in the effort to start earning immediately. Of course, I want you to be realistic about the earnings, but there's no reason for you to think that this won't work. Passive income isn't hard to generate. If you truly understand the ideas mentioned in this book and give it a go, you can do it. With some time, patience and effort, you will soon find yourself on the road to complete financial independence.

I have a favor to ask. If you liked this book, then don't forget to write a review and share the positive note with your friends and family.

Let's hustle together!!